MORE THAN A VILLAGE

MORE THAN A VILLAGE

Raising Black Men in America

CAROLYN BOOKER-PIERCE

J Merrill Publishing, Inc., Columbus 43207
www.JMerrill.pub

Copyright © 2021 J Merrill Publishing, Inc.
All rights reserved. No part of this publication may be reproduced, distributed, or transmitted in any form or by any means, including photocopying, recording, or other electronic or mechanical methods, without the prior written permission of the publisher, except in the case of brief quotations embodied in critical reviews and certain other noncommercial uses permitted by copyright law. For permission requests, contact J Merrill Publishing, Inc., 434 Hillpine Drive, Columbus, OH 43207
Published 2021

Library of Congress Control Number: 2021912423
ISBN-13: 978-1-954414-14-3 (Paperback)
ISBN-13: 978-1-954414-13-6 (eBook)

Title: More Than A Village
Author: Carolyn Booker-Pierce

I dedicate this book to my two sons, Robert and Michael, whom I was blessed to give birth to and raise as black men in America.

I also dedicate this book to my bonus son, Jerry Jr., to who I was fortunate to be his bonus mom while married to his father. I love family and these three African-American men. They are intelligent, funny, and very responsible black men, sons, husbands, and fathers. I am proud to be called their mom.

I appreciate their different personalities and how they all have a way of making me and others feel special. They are very respectful and well-behaved as gentlemen. They have their own gifts and talents that complement who they as human beings.

I wanted to write this book because I have a greater appreciation of who they have become and who they are as black men in America. They are such great men. They are so loving and kind. I knew while raising them as their mother or bonus mother, I would be raising them to be somebody's husband, father, and somebody that needed to be mentally, spiritually, and financially stable. With gratefulness to God and more than a village, they turned out to be all three of the above.

I am so incredibly proud of Robert, Michael, and Jerry Jr. I look forward to seeing how they will affect the world and those who have the pleasure of meeting them in an extraordinary way. They are great leaders of their families and powerful black men.

I want to thank my family village and those who helped influence or raise these wonderful, strong, smart black men. I will be talking about the role they played in this book.

Thanks to all the aunts, uncles, great grandparents, grandparents, teachers, neighbors, churchs, and godparents. Thanks to the employers - past, present, and future.

Thanks to their dads for any positive influences they had on these great young men.

I was a single parent for most of my boys' lives. Still, when I was married, I appreciate the time their bonus dad and dads put into being there physically, emotionally, and financially. My boys' dads gave them what they could at the time, and for that, I am grateful.

CONTENTS

Introduction ix

1. More than a village 1
2. Single Mom 7
3. Bonus Mom 13
4. The Neighborhood 19
5. The Aunts and Uncles 25
6. The Grandparents 31
7. The Church 35
8. The Schools 41
9. The Gangs 45
10. Created equal but Different 49
11. The Talks: Birds and the bees and the Police 55
12. Raising Husbands, Fathers, and Leaders 65
    Notes 73

    About the Author 75
    Also by Carolyn Booker-Pierce 77

Introduction

As a youth, I used to hear it said, it takes a village to raise a child. Well, I believe it takes more than a village. A village consists of what Webster Dictionary describes as,

> A small assemblage of houses in the country, less than a town or city.

Well, all the young men I had the honor to help raise were raised in the city a little larger than the country. It took more than the assembled houses in the neighborhood to raise them. Some of the things that went on in some communities as they got older were not so great. I had to look outside of the village at times for positive influences. I will share more in this book. However, I will try to focus more on the positive things the neighbors and the neighborhoods had to offer the boys as they grew up in and outside their communities.

Having great people, mentors, other men, and family members are essential when it comes to raising black males or any men in America.

If you have seen any of the news during 2020 and 2021, you may understand the reality of what it is like raising black men in America. Racism and police brutality are not new problems. They have been around for as long as I can remember. It is just getting worst and more blatant. As a mother, I sometimes fear if my children would be arrested, killed, or harassed because of the color of their skin.

Having good neighbors, the uncles and aunts, the grandparents, the school programs, the Boys Club, the church, and their fathers all helped influence my sons into becoming the great black men they are today. They are good men, fathers, husbands, and providers. All of which is hard to find amongst African-American men today, but they are out there.

I am sure it helped to have all the right people around them growing up. Their influences helped them navigate through this broken world system. The village and more helped them come out on top and live as healthy black men in America. I believe even the negative influences had great lessons that may have taught them what not to do. In any case, it took more than a village to raise my black men in America.

More than a village

Think about this for a moment.

Who are all those people that helped influence and raise you?

For me, it was my parents, my grandparents, and especially my older sister. None were perfect, neither am I.

They did not always have the best of everything. Still, my parents set a good example of how to be responsible financially. . I can remember drinking Kool-aid was a treat. I saw them work extremely long hours outside of the home to help put food on the table and clothes on our backs. And, there were a lot of mouths to feed in our home.

My siblings and I went to stay with my grandparents in West Virginia every summer. I used to look at it as just a vacation for my siblings and me. Now I can see it was a vacation for my parents. They had a holiday away from all six of their children living in the house at the time. They also had a break from feeding all six of us.

One set of grandparents, my mother's parents, kept us during the week. On the weekend, my father's mother, who lived up the road as we called it, kept us on the weekends. My father's dad was deceased.

I loved going to the country every summer until I felt too grown to stay with my grandparents. If I knew then what I know now, I would have never stopped going to West Virginia every summer. It kept me out of trouble.

The city moved much faster than the country. That means the more years I spent my summers with my grandparents, the further it delayed me from growing up to fast in the city. And that I did.

My grandparents were amazing. There were seven of us children. Six would be there most of the time. They fed all of us very well. And, they kept us neat and clean.

We lived and ate mainly from the farm, fresh meats, and fresh vegetables from the home gardens. The food we ate was freshly cooked. I do not remember eating anything out of the can.

We went to church every Sunday. That was a big tradition in the African-American families in the country and in the city. We learned about God, community, and fellowship in Sunday school and Sunday morning church service. That is where the neighborhood and the village met up every Sunday.

The adults did not see each other much during the week other than to borrow a cup of sugar and holler at each other as they went in and out to buy groceries.

The children in the village, which were primarily relatives, played together daily outside. The adults were busy cooking, cleaning, doing laundry, and other busy work around the houses. Then everyone met up for church fellowship on Sundays. You were going to go to church.

We played with our cousins, who lived all around us, until the sun went. It was a good time and a healthy village to be a part of every summer. Back home, my parents, who worked outside the home, were tired most of the time. We spent a lot of time outside when we were not in school or in the country.

Around age six, my family had moved to a predominately white neighborhood. Thank God as our predominately white neighborhood grew in color, we made more friends to play with and enjoy. All the black families looked out for each other, and we had other family members who lived close by.

One of my uncles, who is like a brother to me and my siblings, would come to take us to his baseball games. He was about the only person our parents allowed us to leave with when we were small children.

At his baseball games, we would get to see and visit with the other family members who were on the team or hanging out at the games. That helped get us out of the yard that we as children were kind of limited to.

I guess that was my father's way of keeping us safe and out of trouble. Still, we thought we were being imprisoned during that time.

Back then, everyone's parent was your parent. If an adult neighbor were to observe you doing something wrong, they would yell at you, and you better not say anything back. Please don't let the neighbors have to call your parents? That would get everything shut down. It was our village. It was our neighborhood, and we respected it.

The same thing happened when you went to school. If you did anything wrong and the teacher had to call our parent/s, it was not good. The school was our home away from home—a lot of lessons are learned in the classroom.

We learned how to sit down and listen. We learned how to read and write. We learned how to respect and get along with others. All of that happened in the classrooms of our schools. That was outside of our neighborhood, the village. Then we went from school to work or to college or the military.

It was more than the neighborhood village that taught us how to live, and we passed that on to our children. I passed what I learned in my village as I raised my black men in America. I learned that they needed those positive influences, and more, in their village to raise them to be strong black men in America.

Single Mom

I became a single mother at seventeen years of age. My oldest son was sixteen years old when I got married for the first time in my thirties. That means for at least sixteen years, I was trying to figure out what raising a black man in American was all about.

The first thing I learned is that I could not do it all by myself. It took the small village around me plus more.

You see, I had my parents who allowed me to live in their home for the first ten years of my first son's life. Not only did I have my parents, but I also had my siblings that were home at the time, who I mentioned in the Dedication.

My neighbors were a blessing too in the community in which I lived. While I took care of things in my life and my firstborn, it helped to have family and good neighbors that would help watch out for him while he would be outside playing with their children or grandchildren.

It was not easy raising my first son as a single mother. He suffered from asthma which involved many nights at Children's Hospital for the first few years of his little life. Because I chose to end the relationship with his father, I did not call on him much during those times. I was very independent and determined that I did not need his father's help. Later, I realized that my son needed him as a father even though I did not need his help. We got on good terms until he moved away.

During that time, his father would visit and pick him up from time to time. After his father relocated, I was back to doing it alone, apart from the help I received from my family. He and his father currently have a great relationship. I am grateful for that. I only wish that there was more time given to him in his earlier days.

Black men need to know and be a part of their father's lives no matter their age. My second son was born nine years later than my first son. I was still single and started out having a similar experience with my second son.

While being raised by a single mother, his father lived closer and had more interaction throughout most of his life. Both still needed a man in their lives consistently.

In my thirties, I got married for the first time. It was great having a man around because I knew there were some things, as a woman, I could not teach or show my young black men about how to be men. My ex-husband was not perfect, neither was I by any means perfect. However, he did bring some balance to the family.

I needed the balance even if the children didn't. I was overly protective of my sons, especially because of them being black men in America. I feared them being ridiculed and harassed because of the color of their skin. I feared them be profile by the police. I feared them being targeted because of the color of their skin.

My ex brought his great sense of humor, patience, and understanding to the family, as well as my bonus son. He helped to balance my fear of letting them go too far out of my sight. Sometimes I felt he was too lenient. Looking back, he was what they needed so I could ease up on those young men even though that was hard for me.

As a single mom, I had no one's opinion in my choices but my own and God's when I would invite him in. When things got rough, and I felt I was failing as a mother, I would quickly call on God. I admit my choices for raising my sons were not always the best, but by God's grace, we made it through.

God always answered my prayers when I did turn to him. I remember when I felt like giving up as a single mother raising one of my sons. God spoke to me in a book written by Bishop T.D. Jakes, "Help I'm Raising My Children Alone." In it, he said something like, God knew I was the only one who could raise my child.

That gave me so much strength and courage to finish the task of being a single mother. If God brought that child to you, surely, he knew you could raise that child. That means if you had or are currently raising your black male child alone, you can, and God knew you would.

Someone may be reading this book and feeling overwhelmed as a single mother or even a married mother. You may need to hear this too. Some married women may feel as though they are raising their child alone because their husband is either gone all the time or not emotionally present. Just know that you are the only one who could raise that child and bring the right influences into that child's life.

That child may be gifted and talented like the one I had to raise. My child came into the world perfectly the way God intended him to come, and so did his brothers.

Be encouraged and know that God is able. God did it for my boys and me. He will do it for you.

My sons give me praise all the time for what I did right as their mother. I know I did not do everything right. They know it too. Still, no one celebrates me better than the men that I had the privilege to help raise. The two sons I gave birth to and my bonus son are the greatest gifts God has ever given me.

God allowed me to be a part of their village. God allowed me to be influential in their lives as black men in America. For that, I am grateful.

Bonus Mom

I don't want to assume everyone knows what a bonus mom or child is. If you don't know what I am referring to when I use the phrase "bonus mom," listen up.

Instead of using the term stepchild or stepparents, the term "bonus" child or parent is a more politically correct phrase to replace the "step." Using the term step is like saying the child or parent is someone less than the biological children or parents. Using the phrase bonus is more like an addition, plus, or a blessing to a family. It is a more positive phrase when referring to children or parents of a blended family.

As I mentioned in the last chapter, I was in my thirties when I got married for the first time. I already had two sons. For a long time, I thought I would never get married due to having children already, but I was wrong.

I got married and inherited a husband and a bonus son. My bonus son was a preteen and already had a mother. It was hard sometimes to know what role I should be playing with a child who already had a mother.

One thing was certain, just like I wanted my ex to love my children as his own, it was equally important that I loved my bonus son as my own. At times I felt he did not care for me because I genuinely treated him as my own. That meant there were rules, and he did not get away with anything just because I was not his birth mother.

My children had to go to school and were expected to make good grades. I expected the same from my bonus son. My children had to be respectful to both parents so did he. My children had to attend church, and he did too. My children had curfews. He had a curfew too. Sometimes I could see how he resented being in the home with me as his bonus mother.

The rules his father and I had in our home were a little different from what he was used to. That really aggravated him.

I loved him regardless. I treated him the same way anyway.

That went on most of the time he lived in the home with me and his dad. When our family was preparing to relocate to another state, I knew he did not want to leave the city he had lived in all his life.

He was so angry and frustrated. He shared with me recently, he had planned to run away from home the night before. I was not surprised because he was that upset about moving. I knew he really was not happy about moving, period. However, he was part of the family and had to go.

The oldest was an adult at the time; therefore, he decided to stay back to live with a family friend. My bonus son and my oldest were close. I sensed he was upset with me more than his father. Although he did not care for the rules in the home, I believe he loved me, if not then now.

He seemed to have grown closer to me the older he got. He shares how what I did for him as a young black male helped him become the man and father he is today to his children and his wife. What a blessing to know that being a part of his more than a village helped cause him to be who he is today. That is a massive compliment on being a bonus parent.

If there are any bonus parents out there feeling frustrated and discouraged dealing with bonus children, hang in there. It will pay off after a while if you treat your bonus children right. It sure did for me.

I love getting calls from my grown bonus child. He does not have to call me. He is free from his bonus mom to do whatever he wants to do now. Instead, he calls me and thanks me. He calls and asks me for advice on raising his children now that he is in a similar situation.

I am so honored to have been a part of his village in and out of the marriage to his father. He is such a great African-American bonus son. I am so proud of him and what he has become as a man, husband, and father.

I am just as proud of my other sons, who I will talk more about later. Remember, if you are a part of a blended family, it takes more than a village to raise children, especially African-American males.

Embrace the gift and opportunity you have been given as a bonus parent. Bonus children can grow up to be a blessing. My bonus son is a blessing, and he is an extension of my village.

The Neighborhood

The neighborhood in Columbus, Ohio, where my children and I were born and raised, used to be a safe place to live. As a child, I remember my family and other middle-class black families moved into the predominantly white neighborhood.

Most of the neighbors were friendly after the transition of blacks moving into the neighborhood. The whites were moving out as though they were running from illegal aliens. The black neighbors grew close, and everybody knew everyone else's families.

The Howards were the only black neighbors that I remember who lived on one side of my family's home when we first moved into the predominantly white neighborhood. They were a friendly middle-class family trying to make a living in a better community while my family was trying to do the same. It was nice having another black family with children around my age who looked like me and were not intimidated by my skin color.

Our families grew up together and are still good friends until this day. I think it went without saying our families had to look out for each other because most whites were sure to let us know we were black, unwanted, and different from them.

That was the time I really understood I was black and different from my white neighbors. An older lady who lived behind us used to call my siblings and the other black families "black birds." She had the nerve to make it into a song. "Black birds, black birds, please fly away."

We named her "Thunderbird" because she would always walk down the back alley drinking Thunderbird alcohol on her way home from the neighborhood store. If you know anything about alcoholics, they do not hold back on how they feel. They will say what is on their heart without remorse or a filter. There were other incidents by other whites in the neighborhood, including their children, that reminded us who we were and our skin color.

But our next-door African-American neighbors and the across-the-street lady we called Grandma would holler at my boys if either of them would ride a bike or big wheel into the street. As my oldest son shared, the neighbors were like family to him. They were like family then and still are like family to this day. The neighbors did not have a problem correcting any of the children in the neighborhood who got out of hand or put themselves in danger.

Unlike the children today, if you try to correct some of them, they are subject to cuss you out. Don't try to report them to some parents. The parents might cuss you out too.

When I was raising my boys, they were taught to respect their elders and their neighbors. They are still just as respectful today as they were coming up in their neighborhoods. If a neighbor asked one of the boys to do a task even if they didn't want to, they would do it without a word.

My oldest son's uncle is two years older than him. Our families were neighbors. That is how I met his dad. The two boys played together and grew up together.

When my son was very sick with asthma, my neighbor would let me use her car to take him to the hospital in the middle of the night. I was a teenage mother who had just gotten my license a year earlier. My neighbor trusted me to use her car until I could purchase my own car a few years later. There were many doctor's appointments and allergy shots that my son had to have. Because of that good neighbor, I was able to make many of those appointments with a toddler without having to catch multiple buses or a cab.

I am grateful for all the neighbors I was blessed to be around growing up, especially those who helped when I was raising my boys. My bonus son shared how he used to go from house to house eating at the neighbor's houses.

One of my sons used to bring seemed like half of the band from school home to visit, and sometimes they would stay all night on the weekends. He would stay the night at one of his friend's homes when I would let him.

Allowing your children to stay at one another's house can be safe if you have met the parent/s. I probably would be even more skeptical today than back in the 1990s. One thing that helped, I got to know the village my children interacted with.

One of my youngest sons decided he wanted to run away from home around age six or seven. I watched as he packed my suitcase to journey off on to God knows where. I thought I would just wait to see what his plan was.

He dragged the packed suitcase out the door and headed across the parking lot of the apartment complex where we were living at the time. I called my neighbor to let her know he was headed her way, and I asked her if she did not mind. I needed her to let it play out with him by asking him some thought-provoking questions about his plans as a runaway.

I told her I would soon come to get him if he did not make his way back across the lot in a little bit. He headed back home about an hour later or so with the packed suitcase after whatever conversation they had. I don't believe much was said as he headed back up the stairs to return to the home he had run away from. I am grateful the neighbor offered a safe place for my little one while he processed that home was across the street with his mother. And his mother would be right there waiting for him to return.

There was somebody in the neighborhood usually looking out for my boys, and I was looking out for other children that I knew as well. That is what more than a village was like for me then and now as part of raising my boys.

That same son loved to wander off, not to run. He just loved people and did not like staying still or at home. When he was old enough to ride a bike, he kept me in terror looking for him.

He would sometimes show up at a childhood friend of mine that I grew up with. He calls her his aunt. She lived several blocks away. I would be frantically looking for him. She was nice enough to eventually give me a call after he had visited with her like he was an adult.

People need other good people to help when a child like my youngest decides they no longer want to hang out at home in their immediate village. Sometimes they just need help from the neighbors in the neighborhood.

The Aunts and Uncles

Thank God for aunts and uncles, at least for the ones my sons had in their lives. My siblings played important parts in helping me to raise my boys.

My oldest son was the first of my parent's grandchildren. I lived with them when he was born and until he was around ten years old. I was young, and most of my siblings were still living at home when he was born.

I had a lot of help from my sisters. My son grew up with my baby sister; therefore, she is more like a sister to him. They bantered back and forth all the time, with him harassing her the most.

He would do things and blame his aunt, like a sister. There was even a house fire he caused, and when the fire department was questioning him, he looked at my baby sister. I looked at him and said, "you better not." Because I knew he was about to blame his aunt. He then told the fireman how the fire got started. He told them he did it playing with a cigarette lighter that belonged to me.

As my sister got older, my son picked up where he left off, harassing his aunt, my baby sister, and her daughter. He started harassing his cousin. Maybe her daughter reminds him of his aunt. I don't know. He may have felt like my sister was getting too old for him to harass, so his poor cousin gets to be bothered with all his harassment.

My baby sister did not live far from us. I would sometimes drop him off to her to babysit him if I had somewhere to go or something to do. My poor niece really became his victim. Every now and then, he still likes to harass my baby sister and, more so, his cousin. He loves them both, and they love him. They are used to his harassment.

Before leaving for the military, my oldest sister was extremely helpful in being part of our village. She hosted my first baby shower to ensure I had everything I needed when my first son was born. She was very encouraging to me as a teenage mother who needed all the help and encouragement I could get. She later inspired me to get a job that I ended up working at for almost 20 years. Her influence helped guide how well I would end up taking care of my children.

She really loved my son and loved entertaining him by eating his sandwiches my little one would make for her back in those days. I could not stomach how the sandwich would look when he finished making them, but my older sister could. The more she ate from him, the prouder he would become, sharing his slimy cookies and anything else he would put in his mouth first and then share with his aunt. Bless her heart. She is such a good aunt. I honestly could not eat anything he put together. It is interesting how picky of an eater he is now.

My sons had no doubt they were both loved by my siblings. My oldest son recalls spending vacation time with his aunt, one of my sisters who lived in Detroit with her husband and family. He shared memories of him and another of my sister's daughters, both visiting at the same time. She has a son that is close to my son's age and the niece that joined them.

It was nice to have siblings that lived in other states my children could visit. My youngest spent some time in Michigan with my sister and her husband as well. Their uncles, my brothers, would pick them up for summer vacations in West Virginia, where my parents are both from.

Both of my sons were fortunate to have met both of their great grandparents on my mother's side and experience the good home cooking and country lifestyle I used to enjoy. They would get picked up by their uncles for summer breaks, giving me the relief required when I had to work overtime to make sure they had everything they needed.

While they may not have liked their village away from home, I sure did. One son says he was taught how to be hospitable by one of his uncles. My other son says their experiences were different.

In any case, I think they both survived their summer vacations in the country. And far as I know, they were safe and came back bigger than what they were when they left.

My youngest son I love dearly; however, he was a challenge to raise. He had his own agenda all the time, and like his mother, his is very independent and strong-willed. We clashed because of that, especially when he was younger.

One thing I didn't understand about his personality then, that I know now, is that he thinks out of the box and is spontaneous. That is what ended up making him the brilliant man he is today. He is very gifted and musically talented. He had a mind of his own that refused to be tamed.

One of my sisters would come and get him every weekend when he was little. Remember, he liked to wander off. She had a lot of patience with him. Besides, she was part of the family village.

She would help me with him by giving me a break on the weekends. In return, I would give her my car to drive the weekend. We were all happy. It worked for all involved. My son was glad to get away with his aunt and get away from me. I was delighted to get a break from him, and my sister had a car to drive all weekend. We all needed each other.

The arrangement worked out perfectly for us. My son said she was like a second mother to him, feeding him and feeding his gift for music. Two of my sisters had children a year after I gave birth to my oldest. I mentioned the one who lived in Detroit. So, my oldest had other children close to him in the home for a while to play with, including the neighborhood children—the more, the merrier.

I did not realize back then how important aunts and uncles were, including their children. However, I can say now I am truly grateful for all their positive influences and the help we gave each other. My youngest was like an only child because his brothers were older than him. But, all the aunts and uncles contributed to being more than a village in raising both of my sons.

There was so much love from them then and now. I needed more than a village raising my sons. My siblings were great at being a part of my and my son's village.

The Grandparents

As I already mentioned, my grandparents, who were my son's great grandparents, played a big part in helping take care of my two African-American sons. They were a big part of their history. They were a part of their extended family village.

My sons could see a two-parent home with them working to provide for themselves and help take care of their children and grandchildren. It costs to feed a family. It cost them to sacrifice their homes while I was trying to get on my feet.

My parents allowed me to stay at home way longer than I should have. It was mainly my mother that let me stay so long. My father, who knew that I needed to at some point get out of their house, finally gave my children and me the boot I needed.

It was the best thing that ever happened to my children and me. We needed and had our own space, and we had our own new neighborhoods. Once I moved out, I took full responsibility for taking care of my two children alone, except when I was married.

My parent's home provided a safe place for me to raise my children. When I lived there, most of the good neighbors were still there. I did not pay hardly any rent for a long time.

My oldest son was able to take away some of my dad's, as well as my own, business sense. When he was around ten, we moved out of my parent's house. He was able to see my father go to work and buy the groceries on payday and do it consistently. He saw my father and mother work hard. My mother would bring home what my father may have forgotten. Sometimes they would bring home the same thing.

He saw my father retire after working over forty years at the same place. He said his grandfather influenced him with his work ethic and how to take care of a family. I believe my oldest is a lot like my father when handling finances and anything having to do with money. He is savvy when it comes to saving money, like his grandfather. He is smart with how he spends his money, like his grandfather. He is thoughtful about being the same kind of an example with his son, my grandson. I am so proud of how he has turned out, with my father as the main man he has spent most of his young life growing up around.

My mother was a big help with putting my son on the daycare bus that came after my leaving for work. If she had not been there to put him on the daycare bus, I would have been late for work or had to make other arrangements. It was so much easier for me to have his grandmother put him on the daycare bus.

His grandmother was very helpful when I had to take care of business or work late. She and my dad were part of their grandchildren's village. They were a blessing and a vital part of my son's village, especially my oldest. My youngest was a baby when I finally moved out of my parent's home. However, both sons have had their own personal experience of knowing their grandparents.

My bonus son shared how his maternal grandmother was influential in sharing her faith and spirituality. He says she showed him love and how to love. I think that is true for most of the grandparents. They are good for showing their grandchildren love. I am genuinely grateful for the grandparents being a part of my sons' village.

The Church

I became a born-again believer just before my twenty-first birthday. My oldest was around three and a half years old. Thank God because I was still headed in the wrong direction. I could have easily let my negative behaviors before being a believer influence the young man I was raising. Instead, I started going to church and took my son to church.

It was my hope that he and later his brothers would find the same joy of being in a relationship with the God that answered my prayers. I can remember how overwhelmed I had become trying to figure out how to take care of my son as a teenaged mother.

After becoming a born-again believer, I found myself at the altar for prayer often. It was prayer at home and at the altar that healed my son from asthma. He really struggled those first three and a half years of his life. I could not work until he started getting better due to spending so much time at the hospital, doctor's appointments, and taking him to get allergy shots. He has not had any trouble with asthma since those early years. Most people don't fully recover from asthma, but he did.

When my second child was born - the one with all the energy and knew how to work my last nerve. I used to take him to the altar and have him prayed over. I used to fear him getting into trouble being a young black man because he would always say what he thought. He was kind of aggressive in his younger years. As he was getting older as a teenager, I would just go up for prayer for him. It finally paid off. Now he is one of the most wonderful and amazing men I know.

The church became a priority for me and my house. That part of our village got me through a lot of rough times. Being an active member of a community of faith-filled believers helped change my life from the old person I used to be, as well as my son. I can also see how faith and the church have helped shape the character of all my sons' lives.

In the beginning, they were not fans of church. The youngest was the only fan of church-going because he loved being around people, and he loved music. However, I would have never thought he would be this invested in church looking back in his early years.

He has always been the most social of the bunch. He loved to sing and sang well. Because of his love for music, he was in the children's choir by the age of four. Rules were broken at the church we attended to allow him to sing in the children's choir, which typically started at age five. He developed such a love for the church organ. With the influence of the organ player, he is now a minister of music himself.

You never know how much bringing a child to church can influence the child in the future in such a positive way. Even my two other sons, which include my bonus son, say that the church gave them their faith and desire to love and serve God on their own today.

In the beginning, the two of them hated going to church growing up. However, I believe the church has been one of my sons' biggest positive influences on having faith and knowing where to turn to for spiritual guidance and help. Unlike people, the good news of the gospel never changes.

Prayer is always a source of continued comfort, and God has not failed them or me up until this point. I have found hope in the church and in prayer when times were hard raising my boys, especially when I was a single mother.

I used to host a women's home Bible Study when I was married, which provided a positive community for my sons and me. As the adults were on one floor having our spiritual fellowship, the children would gather in our basement to eat, laugh and play. It was a good and healthy way for the women and their children from different churches and non-church-going families to come together for the same purpose, to love on each other, learn more about faith, and give our children an opportunity to be around other children. The children used to enjoy the women's fellowship night mainly because there was a lot of food that came with it.

The Church was an extension of our village that helped keep me and my sons encouraged and grounded positively. We all still traditionally use our faith in God and the church to positively influence our lives. It was the church and the grace of God that helped me to raise my black male sons. After working all week, I could be totally worn out dealing with things that may have gone on at their schools, out of school, and in the home that made me tired or stressed. Once I made it to a good old-fashioned church service, I would return home refreshed, ready to start my week of dealing with home, my sons, work, and life again.

One of the elders of the church I used to attend was very helpful with being a part of my youngest son's village. If you may have noticed, my youngest had a lot of energy, and he was the most challenging to raise. I needed all the help I could get from the neighborhood village and the extended church village. The elder, who he called grandpa, helped to keep him entertained. Later, I found out this same elder started giving him driving lessons around fourteen years old. That was a great example of how things were supposed to be done, right? And yes, I am being sarcastic.

In any case, my son spent a lot of time with this elder and another young African-American single mother's son. The elder would pick up both boys to spend time with him on the weekends. He fed them well and gave them the kind of attention and support they needed from an older man.

During that time, there was not a man consistently in either of their lives. This elder, whom I was very fond of, is now deceased. However, he was an excellent extension of me and my youngest son's village at the time. I appreciate all the times he spent with my son, and I miss him a lot. He was someone whom I could confide in regarding things my son may have been going through.

Every black male raised by a single parent needs a man of faith from their local church or a positive mentor to help raise or spend time with their sons. They need male influences as an extension to the family village. The church was a significant influence on my sons and me.

It took more than my family village. It took more than a village to help raise my sons. It took faith in God, the church, and the people of God willing to be a part of my and my sons' lives.

The Schools

I found it interesting that upon interviewing my sons, bonus son included, they all hated school for the most part. After hearing what they all had to say, I am grateful that any of them graduated.

I was mainly surprised that the oldest, an A and B student, most of his days attending school, said he hated high school. Then he explained he started hating school in his senior year. That is when I noticed a change in his grades for the first time since he was a kindergartener.

For the other two, I was not surprised that they hated school. I was just surprised at how much they hated school and did not care if they graduated or not.

While they may or may not see the benefit of school, period. When it comes to being black men in America, I felt then, and now, they must understand their odds of being chosen for employment usually fall at the bottom of the list compared to their white counterparts. The less education they have, the further down the list they may go.

Like it or not, when a person already has 'being black' as a strike against them, being uneducated and black is like having three more strikes against them. People can pretend the color of a person's skin does not matter in the workplace, and education does not play a part in the selection process, but that is not the truth.

I have been working since I was around 15 years old. I have watched my white counterparts move up the ladder, including some with less education, move quicker than I have and those of my race. It is a difference. True, that may not happen everywhere. However, it occurs in a lot of places.

I have seen it take longer for my sons to get hired or get a promotion than their white counterparts, and one has a master's degree. The color of my son's skin and their education can make a difference.

I am so proud of whatever level of education my sons received because they went to school even when they hated it. The school is where they got their first and most important education outside of the home, as I mentioned earlier.

The school is where they first began to learn life skills starting in kindergarten, and it is a part of the extended village whether children or adults like it or not.

The Gangs

As a mother, I always tried to pay attention to my son's behavior that would signal a significant change. I worked with youth at a local drug treatment facility in the early 2000s.

During that time, I was very aware of the colors worn by certain gang members. I had to have some level of safety and control in my substance abuse group classrooms. There was the red against the blue colors. It was the Bloods against the Crips.

I could tell by body language as soon as I had one or more opposing gang members in the same room. Tensions would arise, and I would have to make a statement that they would not be one against the other in my classroom. A red or blue bandana, a type of scarf, was not allowed to be worn or hidden under pants legs, on the wrist, or under shirts. Not on my time, not in my class. Some would try me. Then, I started collecting them from those who showed up after warning them in my substance abuse class.

I did not notice any major changes in behaviors with my sons while they were under my roof. However, I was made aware of several occasions when my sons were either approached or had statements made that let my sons know who the gang members were.

One son said while visiting his grandparents, one of the young men who moved in next door asked him not to wear a particular color shirt. When I asked him, what his response was, he said rather nonchalantly, "I took it off." My son also said he did not tell me because he did not want me to panic.

I am so glad he did not tell me. He knew his mother and how protective I was of him and his brothers. I think he handled it much better than I would have.

I remember another son sharing how he and a friend had stopped at a neighborhood car wash to wash his car. He wore a red shirt that day. He said

THE GANGS

some gang members approached him and his friend asking, "What up?"

My son was clueless until the guys indicated they thought they were representing an opposing gang because of the color of his shirt. That could have gone badly for my son and his friend had they not let the guys know that they weren't a part of a gang. They were glad to walk away from that awkward situation.

It became a thing, whereas I would ask my sons not to wear certain colors like red or blue to avoid being identified as a gang member in certain neighborhoods. It was another one of those things that needed to be addressed being a black male in America.

My sons appeared to have survived the peer pressures surrounding them in their neighbors, schools, and other places like the car wash. Another son shared when he was invited to join a gang, they told him they would be like a family to him. He was told they did not rob or steal only to find out that was not true.

There are so many circumstances that challenged them as black men and me as a mother trying to encourage them to be safe. Prayer was my best weapon of defense because there was no way I could be with them all the time.

They seemed to know what to do when approached by gang members. However, I knew I could not protect them from all the things, the choices, and challenges the world had waiting for them as black men in America, gangs being one of them.

Being raised in a Christian home had a lot to do with them surviving the gang scene, whether they were a part of a gang or not. At least, I believe it has.

Created equal but Different

All three of the sons have different personalities while created equally. All were created by God, and all were created black men. It took me a while to figure out why my first son is so much different in his personality than the other two. He is laid back, has a quiet spirit, easy-going as well as compliant. I later learned he has a Phlegmatic type personality temperament. Jenna Birch, in her September 3, 2019, Well and Good article on, "What's Your 'Temperament'?" writes,

> Phlegmatic types are the likable peacemakers who are calm, cool, collected, and diplomatic above all else. They care a lot about others, but are also emotionally reserved and hide their feelings from those they care

about. They are relaxed and rarely ruffled, easily able to explain complex problems to others, and they are great empathizers. Phlegmatics fly under the radar and don't draw attention to themselves, preferring the intimacy of close friends and the solitude of their alone time.

That describes my oldest son better than I could. He is very easy to be around because he is calm, pleasant, and an introvert like me, his mother. He is the only one who is introverted like me. I wish I had as calm of a personality as he has. Some people say I do, but this son really knows how to chill. I tend to worry and be a little anxious at times.

Because of my oldest's calm and pleasant demeanor, he tends to bring that same calm to any atmosphere. He is an absolute joy to be around. He is so reserved it is sometimes hard to tell when things are troubling him. He enjoys his solitude the same way I do. Therefore, I just check in with him if I sense something is wrong. He will usually give me a nonchalant answer. We both like numbers, and both have or have had careers in accounting. After 20 years, I gave up numbers, and currently, he is still going strong as an accountant.

My son second has a Sanguine-type personality. He is usually the life of the party, totally opposite of my first. He does not meet any strangers and knows how to work a crowd or a small group of people. He is a people person and has a larger-than-life-good personality to go with it. Most people love him because of his big and charming personality. He can either bring a smile to my face with his fun sense of humor and charisma, or he can make me nervous from being too loud.

He thinks it is hilarious that he can get on my nerves like that. It used to really drive me crazy. However, I now understand that it is just his personality that is different from his older brother and myself. I would not change him for the world because his Sanguine-type character brings balance to the probably too quiet of a personality his brother and I can bring. His friendly personality is a joy to be around, and he keeps us going when he is around. Jenna says this about the Sanguine type personality,

> *Sanguine personalities are bright, optimistic, cheerful, energetic, and spontaneous. They embody youth and are easily bored, preferring constant entertainment to sitting still. They prefer variety to stability, and often chase risk with a high tolerance for adventure. They tend to be very friendly and easy to be around, but they don't always take things seriously.*

That is an accurate description of my second son. He is very bright full of wisdom. His energy was always a challenge for me. I am not what you would consider spontaneous, but he is. He has what he calls random thoughts he likes to share personally and publicly. His random thoughts that he freely shares are without a filter and sometimes cause me to cringe. That is why so many people from our village were needed in his life to help me out.

He really doesn't take things too seriously. I could be totally irritated with him, and he will be hysterically laughing. That type of behavior will either aggravate you or cause you to laugh too. In my latter years, I have learned to lighten up and laugh with him. His cheerfulness, while it can sometimes seem offensive, is what makes people like to be around him. I currently have a greater appreciation for his personality than I did when he was that annoying little child disappearing in the neighborhood that I had to look for in the village.

He thought it was no big deal as he would spontaneously disappear. I would be hysterical. His big personality has gotten him a lot of positive connection in the church community and the job where we both work; imagine that. That is because he is so personable and knows how to get people's attention in a way that benefits him. He is not afraid to be himself, and for that, I am proud of him. He really does have a great personality and cares about people, especially me, his mother.

Now my bonus son is a little hard to peg. He is, I believe, between the Phlegmatic and the Melancholy personalities. He is more like the Phlegmatic with a laid-back personality. He tends to lean toward an easy-going and calm temperament. He is very caring and relaxed. He is not loud at all but enjoys people and, at the same time, quiet. He is analytical like the Melancholy temperament and takes things to heart. He is very talented in the arts and media and is a real family man. I am so proud of the man he has become.

I bring up the temperaments because I learned I had to deal with each of my sons based on their different personalities. The oldest, I only had to tell him to do something once, and he had no problem complying. He did not like ruffling any feathers. He did not need much discipline.

The youngest son, when dealing with him, was a whole different story, totally different personality. I had to tell him a hundred times, threaten him, punish him, and he still did not listen. Remember, he was the Sanguine of the bunch. If it wasn't fun or exciting, he did not take me or anyone else seriously.

While he was quiet and laid back, my bonus son was somewhat like the youngest son when they were younger. All of them have fun-loving personalities. While the youngest was loud with his protest, my bonus son was quiet with his. He wouldn't say anything. He just wouldn't do anything he didn't want to do. I had to yell at one and talk to the other to keep them motivated as young black men.

Now they all have grown up, still created differently, and loved equally. I still get pretty much the same response out of them but in a more respectful way. Now I understand that they are not deliberately trying to give me grief. I am seeing them as people with their own personalities as equal but different smart black men. I can see a little of the family genetics from their family villages playing out in each of them and their individual personality types from the four temperaments.

The Talks: Birds and the bees and the Police

The birds and the bees talk.

My sons probably knew more than I did about sex when they were coming up. Still, as a mother, I knew I needed to shed some light. Still, I was not sure how or if I should give my sons "The Talks." The talk was supposed to consist of how to handle yourself when it comes to having a sexual life and pregnancy.

When is it time to have a talk? You know when you can visibly see your young boys moving into adolescence. They don't want you to see them in their little underwear like they have something to hid. However, you respect their privacy when they run to their bedroom from the shower with a towel tightly wrap around their underdeveloped bodies.

When you start to notice them staring at little girls longer and harder, they can't hear you talking to them for them staring. They begin to get this lustful look in their eyes - just a lot of staring and looks of discomfort when the girls come around. Suddenly they have no interest in the fellows they used to ride big wheels and bikes with.

As they become teenagers and hormones are all over the place. They become secretive when they talk on the phone. You or a man, if in the house, better have the talk.

I remember one of my sons decided he would cut school with his new girl crush. I had just starting to notice his sudden interest in the opposite sex. His godmother let me know he had asked her to drop him off at a female's house when he and she should have been in school.

Honestly, I about freaked out when I found out he had spent the whole day alone with a female while he should have been in school. I feared he had unprotected sex and the girl would get pregnant. I thought about what I was going to say as I waited for him to return home.

Well, my talk ended up being very brief and to the point. I told him I knew where he had been all day. Then I told him if he got the girl pregnant, he would have to give her his whole check to take care of the baby. He had a job, and he liked having his own money. He looked like a deer in headlights, terrified of what I had just said. We never had another talk about getting a girl pregnant. Years later, he told me it scared him enough that he did not want to do anything to get a girl pregnant and became very careful from that point on.

Another son fell "head over heels," so to speak, for what we used to call a "fast girl." This young lady who would come to the house and stay so late we had to take her home, or she would not leave. My son seemed like he was losing his grip over her, and he was still in high school trying to finish, but this young lady clearly had all his attention. She was starting to be at the house all the time. I was married, hoping after I told my husband to have the talk with him that he would get a grip.

He was totally infatuated with this girl. I did not want to hurt her feelings by telling her to stay away, so I prayed that they would lose interest or that she would move away. Well, she ended up moving to another state. Now the running joke is don't bring the new girl around. If mom thinks she is not the right one, she will pray her away.

My bonus son is another quiet one. He went under the radar until his children started being born. Because he was so quiet, I never had the talk or didn't think he needed a talk or prayer, but I guess he did. He has produced the most children, and they are all beautiful.

Whatever way you choose to talk with your black men about sexual relationships, make sure you encourage them to be responsible men. That is one thing that is clear that happened with the examples or talks with the black males I had the pleasure of helping to raise. They all are responsible black men and fathers to their children or lack of children.

THE TALKS: BIRDS AND THE BEES AND ...

The Police.

I remember giving "warning talks" to help my young black males avoid getting pulled over by the police. When one of my sons began to drive, he liked to play his music loud throughout our predominantly white neighborhood. He also liked to ride around with a car full of his so-called high school friends, who were also black males. I could understand his need to have friends and identify with the other black males who attended high school. However, I have been in American long enough to know if you want to avoid being targeted by the police, you should try to avoid doing the following:

1) don't be a black male (which for my sons is impossible)

2) don't rid around with your music blasting (which I had warned my son)

3) don't ride around with a car full of mischievous young males, especially black males (which I had warned my son earlier the same day) and

4) don't ride around with the taillight out on your car in order to play your speakers loud because you can't run both at the same time (I did not know that was happening until he was pulled over).

One of the officers said the taillight is what initially got my son pulled over. I believe the loud music, then the car full of young black males initially drew the officer's attention. And the taillight gave them a reason to pull my son over. It happens all the time to other black males. The police would have a car full of young black males pulled over. One of the young men who had marijuana on him almost got my son sent to jail. The office said had he not seen the young man throw the marijuana on the floor of my son's car, my son would have gone to jail instead of his friend. While my talk about getting pulled over at first went unheard. I never knew of that son getting pulled over for any of those reasons after that incident.

Then his younger brother got his license and had just driven me somewhere and was driving a little too fast. I warned him not to drive so fast so that he would not get pulled over. He let me out of the car, totally ignoring what I have just said, pulling off speeding. Not 20 minutes later, he called saying he had gotten pulled over by the police and received his first speeding ticket. It was not that my sons were doing any serious crimes that I was worried about. It was the fear of how they would be treated as young black African-Americans if pulled over by the police. African-American males are more likely to not only get pulled over by the police but be arrested and incarcerated at a rate higher than white males doing the same type of crime.

In Bruce Drake's Pew Research Center 2013 article, Incarceration gap widens between whites and blacks,

Black men were more than six times as likely as white men to be incarcerated in federal and state prisons, and local jails in 2010, the last year complete data are available, according to a Pew Research Center analysis. That is an increase from 1960, when black men were five times as likely as whites to be incarcerated.

One of my sons I warned about hanging around people from his old neighborhood. While I tried to protect him from going to jail, he ended up going not only to jail but to prison because he did not listen, just like neither of his brothers when I tried to warn them. Even today, fathers and mothers need to warn their black males how to respond when being pulled over by the police.

a) Don't give the police a reason to pull you over

b) Put your hands where the police can see them

c) Don't reach for anything unless you alert the police officer of what you are reaching for

d) Don't be mouthy with the police

e) If you feel you are being treated unfairly, wait until you are in court or have legal representation to make your case.

After doing all the above, a black male will still be profiled and targeted by the police. I know it is not all police who target black males. I work for law enforcement, so I understand that some good people are not targeting or mistreating black males. The reality is, if you watched the news lately, there are more black males being killed by police than whites. More black males are being arrested than whites, and they are both committing the same kind of crimes.

It is important because the police are a part of my sons' and other black men's villages. Everyone should be treated with the same level of respect when being arrested or pulled over. Our neighborhoods and villages need to be able to trust the police when being pulled over or called upon.

I should not, nor should any other mothers or fathers, fear our black sons being targeted or killed by the police who have a duty to protect and serve.

But it is something that I pray about in hopes that one day things will change so our neighborhoods, villages, and black men can feel and be safe when dealing with the police.

Raising Husbands, Fathers, and Leaders

I have already mentioned as a mother, I was protective of my sons. I was protective of the reality that any one of them could fall prey to drug addiction, jail or prison, or anything that would cause them not to succeed. I wanted to protect my sons from anything that would hinder them from being good husbands, fathers, and leaders. Most importantly, I did not want them to be restricted from becoming the best they could be as black males in American.

I know and understand, especially now that there were some things that I just can't protect my sons from. They all had to grow up by learning from their mistakes. I knew I could not teach my sons everything that a man could. However, I knew I could influence them in the best positive way possible as their mother.

I felt very proud when my oldest told me that I prepared him to be a responsible man and how to deal with things in life during his younger years. He said I influenced him as a father going through a divorce, giving him advice and encouraging him to be a father to his son during our conversations. He also shared that he was influenced spiritually. Being in church at an early age instilled in him a routine that he carries until this day. It was important as a mother when they came along that I understood I was raising somebody's husband, father, employee, and leader. Therefore, spirituality and other positive influences such as work, school, and church, I knew I had to be a good example.

It was important that my sons went to school at a young age, got a job as soon as possible, and learned how to manage their money. My oldest son shared with me just recently that while on vacation with his aunt and uncle in Detroit, he worked in their convenience store for free. He had to have been in early adolescence. He said he learned to work the cash register, tag items, and restocked items on shelves. He also gladly shared how he was able to eat the food in the store as he worked. I guess that was his pay.

What an amazing opportunity he was given while spending vacation time with part of his family village. He started working his first paying job around 15 years of age. He had things he could put on his resume I knew not of but may have helped get and keep his first paying job at a grocery store.

He has been working consistently since then. He currently is an accountant and has always loved numbers, making and saving money. As mentioned earlier, he watched his grandfather work hard. His grandfather had signs of saving money all in his room. He had jars with coins he was saving. He had rolls of coins lying around in plain sight that were constantly growing. His grandfather never lacked money once he got his feet above water.

He saw his grandmother sometimes working two jobs because we lived with my parents until he was ten. I started working when I was about 15 years of age. I stopped during the time he was sick. When he was well, I continued to work.

As shared earlier, I had a career in accounting, just as my son does now. He was shown a strong work ethic from the time he was a child. Now he has the same strong work ethic. He is a stellar dad to his son, not because he is my son. He is setting an excellent example for his son, who is also good at math and numbers.

My grandson is already like my son and his great grandfather when it comes to money. He knows how to save money and not spend every dime he has. They hang out together and have a great bond that my son was not privileged to have with his father in his early years. My oldest was sixteen when I got married the first time. By that time, he had primarily been exposed and influenced by my father, whom my son says did not talk much, which he did not. My father showed him by example how to work hard. He retired after working 40 plus years at a steel plant to provide for his family. My son learned by this example and is working to help provide for his family.

My youngest is still a newlywed. He recently got married to his wife. I am proud of the way he is building his future as a husband and a provider. He had followed in my footsteps on the job working for corrections. He has multiple influences, such as my dad and his father. He says his biological father influenced him regarding working hard and taking care of his family. He would see his father shopping for him and his other siblings. He would spend summers and holidays with his dad. He knew his father took care of him financially. He says his bonus dad encouraged him to respect and have a good relationship with me, his mother. I appreciate that positive influence and aspect of my ex when I was married to him. He never allowed the children to disrespect me regardless of whatever went on with us in our home or in the relationship.

I am impressed at how well my son is doing as a husband and a provider of his family. He has multiple streams of income. The men in his life, for the most part, were positive influences throughout his life. One thing I noticed about my youngest, he is a giver. He has no problem be a blessing to others. He always asks me if I need anything. He says it from his heart. I know if I needed anything that he would freely give it if he has it. I like that about him. His brothers will do the same. He doesn't mind looking out for his mother. Therefore, it is no surprise he has no problem taking care of his wife.

It was important that he saw his father taking care of his family. He was not selfish in his giving as well. Black males need to see their fathers actively taking care of their children. They never know who is watching, especially their children.

My bonus son has really made me proud, and I am sure his biological parents proud, by the way. He is a good husband to his wife and father to his children. As I watch how they interact with each other, I know that he is present as a father and husband. He takes pride in taking his children to school, doctor, and dentist appointments. It is a joy to watch him as a responsible black man. I believe that he does his best to financially provide for his family, and that is important. However, there is nothing more important than for a father to be present in a child's life. He is very present in his children's lives. That is priceless and more meaningful. I can tell he really loves his wife and children, and they really love him.

As his bonus mother, he says I showed him motherly love. And for that, I am grateful because he is such a lovable person and was hard not to love when we all lived together. I am not surprised his family loves him like they do. He says his father helped him believe what a family was supposed to look like. He says anytime he went through something, his dad always connected him with prayer. He says he still calls him for guidance.

As leaders, I believe all three of the boys considering the times they live in, are all doing exceptionally well. As long as my sons do their part as good husbands, fathers, and leaders in their villages, other dynamics outside of the village will help shape their families to be great, especially the black sons they are raising.

I am so glad my sons are very active fathers. Hopefully, as fathers, they get to have the same great experiences and outcomes as I have had raising them as black males in America. That does not mean they will not have their ups and downs. They may have some good times and some bad. However, by allowing the right people to be a part of their village, their black sons can grow up to be great black men like their fathers have become.

Always remember it takes more than a village to not only raise black men but children, period. Since my only experience was with raising black males, that is all I could really talk about. I am glad about my experience. It taught me that it is possible to raise black men in America in marriage or as a single parent. They can come out just fine with a whole lot of prayer and a whole lot of different people—more than a village.

Notes

Websters Definition of Village http://www.webster-dictionary.net/definition/village

Jakes, T.D, "Help I'm Raising My Children Alone," Charisma House, 1996

Incarceration gap widens between whites and blacks, By Bruce Drake, September 6,2013

Jenna Birch, September 3, 2019, Well and Good Article, What's Your 'Temperament'? Meet the Ancient Greek Personality System That Uses, Um, Bodily Fluids, https://www.wellandgood.com/temperament-psychology/

About the Author

Carolyn Booker Pierce is a licensed social worker, teacher, mentor, and spiritual leader born and raised in Columbus, Ohio.

After leaving a career of almost 20 years in accounts payable and claims auditing, Carolyn followed her passion in the area of social services. She then graduated with a BA at Capital University to become a licensed social worker. Carolyn gravitates to chemical dependency counseling as a substance abuse group and individual counselor.

Later she took her years of experience as a substance abuse counselor into her local county jail to serve inmates struggling with substance abuse, alcoholism, and family relationship problems. She is known for listening to others without judgment as they process their everyday life problems.

Carolyn desires to help people grow, heal from their past, and move on to a healthy future. She enjoys spending time with her family, church worship center, traveling, writing, and empowering others.

facebook.com/carolyn.pierce.5245

Also by Carolyn Booker-Pierce

Because the Lord is My Shepherd: Psalm 23 and Me

Girl, You're Not Crazy. You're Dealing With a Narcissist

Loving the Addict: While Taking Care of Yourself First

Abortion!: George and Giovanna